AND Mort Walker

Here we see the two people most responsible for the success of **Beetle Bailey**—Beetle himself and his famous creator, Mort Walker, as caricatured by fellow artist Emory Clark. Walker's artful genius and wry humor have catapulted his reluctant army private to international stardom and popularity. One of the most successful comic strips in the history of comics, **Beetle Bailey** is syndicated in nearly 1,100 newspapers and enjoyed by more than 50 million readers in the U.S. and 43 other countries. It has also won every major prize awarded by the comics profession.

Artist Walker sees Beetle and his buddies as a "U.S. Army made up primarily of civilians. Beetle is typical of these civilians who never become real soldiers. He resists this unnatural way of life in every way he can."

Mr. Walker's life, on the other hand, is perfectly natural. Married, with seven children (five boys and two girls), he lives and works in Greenwich, Conn., where he also writes and produces several other nationally known strips, among them **Hi and Lois,** and **Boner's Ark.**

Fall Out Laughing,

beetle bailey®

by MORT WALKER

tempo books

GROSSET & DUNLAP

PUBLISHERS • NEW YORK

PUBLISHED SIMULTANEOUSLY IN CANADA

LIBRARY OF CONGRESS CATALOG CARD NUMBER: 69-17643

TEMPO BOOKS IS REGISTERED IN THE U.S. PATENT OFFICE

ISBN: 0-448-12134-4

A TEMPO BOOKS **Original**

PRINTED IN THE UNITED STATES OF AMERICA

SOME OF THE GANG AT CAMP SWAMPY

KILLER DILLER

SGT. ORVILLE SNORKEL

ZERO

LT. SONNY FUZZ

COOKIE

PLATO

CAPT. SAM SCABBARD

GEN. AMOS. T. HALFTRACK

CHAPLAIN STANEGLASS

BEETLE, SOME DAY YOU'RE GONNA BE SORRY YOU SAID THAT
OH, YEAH?! WHAT DAY?! NAME THE DAY!
WHAT DAY AM I GONNA BE SORRY? WHAT DAY?!

WHAT'S THE DATE, PLATO?
MORT WALKER

SARGE, I THINK IT'S TIME I GOT PROMOTED
WHAT MAKES YOU THINK YOU'RE BETTER THAN ANYONE ELSE?
1-16

WHAT ABOUT ROCKY? ZERO? COSMO? KILLER?
PROMOTE THEM TOO

© King Features Syndicate, Inc., 1968. World rights reserved.
DID YOU GET AN ANSWER ?
NO, BUT HE ENJOYED THE QUESTION
HA
HOHO
GASP
HAHAHA
HEE
HO
HO
HEE
HA
MORT WALKER

COOKIE LOOKS TERRIBLE
I'LL SAY! HE HAD A MEDICAL CHECKUP YESTERDAY
11-6
© King Features Syndicate, Inc., 1968. World rights reserved.

AND THE DOCTOR TOLD HIM TO CUT DOWN ON STARCHES
MORT WALKER

HOOOoo
HOOOoo
IS THAT SARGE'S SIGNAL ?
BETTER WAIT TILL WE'RE SURE. WE DON'T WANT TO FOUL UP THE ATTACK

HOO HOO, YOU IDIOTS! HOO HOO!!
THAT'S HIM
MORT WALKER 10-31
© King Features Syndicate, Inc., 1968. World rights reserved.

WHAT'LL I DO, SARGE?! SHOULD I GET A ROPE? DO I NEED TO FILL OUT A FORM FOR ONE? HOW ABOUT GETTING SOME GUYS WITH A NET BELOW?
OH, FOR TH--

WHY DON'T YOU BUILD ME A GOLDEN STAIR AND I'LL WALK DOWN!!
MORT WALKER

TAP TAP TAP TAP
7-2

NOW, WHERE DID SARGE GO?
8-1
MORT WALKER

DO YOU STILL WANT THAT DOUBLE SHAKE?

MENU
POT ROAST
LIMA BEANS
POTATOES BEETLE
PIE, LEMON.
"POTATOES BEETLE?" WHAT'S THAT?

POTATOES THAT ARE PEELED POORLY
MORT WALKER
2-27
© King Features Syndicate, Inc., 1968. World rights reserved.

ZERO, I'M GOING OVER TO THE PX. WHILE I'M GONE I WANT YOU TO LOOK OUT FOR THINGS. FOLLOW ME?
YOU BET, SARGE

I KNEW WHEN I SAID IT I DIDN'T PHRASE IT RIGHT
PX
2-2
MORT WALKER

LOOK! SARGE IS WAITING UP TO HEAR ALL ABOUT YOUR DATE
AW, WHY DOESN'T HE GET A DATE OF HIS OWN?
Z
5-24

THE WAY YOU TELL IT IS BETTER THAN THE REAL THING!
DO YOU THINK SO?
Z Z Z Z Z Z Z Z Z
MORT WALKER

IT WON'T BE LONG TILL THEY BUILD UP A HUGE STOCKPILE
WHAT CAN WE DO?
CHINA TESTS H-BOMB

FORE!
2-15
MORT WALKER

IS HE SULKING ON THAT STUPID ROOF AGAIN? I KNOW HOW TO GET HIM DOWN!
MESS HALL

YOU WANNA KNOW THE TRUTH?! YOU'RE A **LOUSY** COOK! THERE'S NOT ONE SINGLE THING YOU COOK RIGHT! WHAT DO YOU SAY TO **THAT**?!

© King Features Syndicate, Inc., 1968. World rights reserved.
Mort Walker
2-14

SOME PARTY LAST NIGHT! I'LL BET SARGE IS FEELING TERRIBLE
YEAH. HE SAYS HIS TONGUE IS A BIT FUZZY

HA! HA! WELL, THERE'S NOT MUCH HE CAN DO ABOUT THAT **NOW**
2-6
MORT WALKER
© King Features Syndicate, Inc., 1968. World rights reserved.

ALL THE ACOUSTICAL WORK IS DONE, GENERAL
GOOD! NOW I WON'T BE DISTRACTED BY ALL THE OFFICE CHATTER

1-23

CHAPLAIN, WHAT DO THE MEN REALLY THINK OF ME?
OH.. ER ..UH...
12-27

THEY THINK OF YOU AS THEIR **FRIEND!** SOMEONE WHO IS KIND AND FAIR AND CONSIDERATE

MORT WALKER

PREPAREDNESS IS IMPORTANT! BEFORE A UNIT MOVES INTO THE JUNGLE, WHAT MUST IT BE SURE TO DO?
JUNGLE SURVIVAL
1 CHECK
3 TEST
1-11

THROW A PARTY FOR THE HELICOPTER PILOTS!
© King Features Syndicate, Inc., 1968. World rights reserved.
MORT WALKER

HOW MANY PIECES OF PIE DID YOU HAVE, SARGE?
ONE

SPRONG

HOW MANY ?!
MORT WALKER

PHLUMP
BA-LUMP
OH-OH! SARGE LEFT THE TEN PIN STANDING
12-16
© King Features Syndicate, Inc., 1967. World rights reserved.

TEMPORARILY
MORT WALKER

THE CAPTAIN JUST TOLD THE GENERAL THAT EACH GUY IN THE COMPANY HAS A SPECIAL ABILITY
HE SAID I SHINE AT FIGURING OUT EASIER WAYS TO DO THINGS

AND HE SAID LT. FUZZ SHINES AT BEING ALWAYS READY AND EAGER TO LEARN

WHERE DID HE SAY I SHINE?
STAND UP AND I'LL SHOW YOU
MORT WALKER

THERE'S A WAC OUT THERE IN SHOCK, DOCTOR
WHAT HAPPENED?
10-29

SHE WAS GOING BY "A" COMPANY JUST AS SGT. SNORKEL WAS BAWLING OUT A PLATOON
MORT WALKER

WELL! I'M GLAD TO SEE ONE PERSON HAPPILY CHEWING AWAY!

WHAT IS IT? THE CREAMED PARSNIPS..? THE CARROT PATTIES...? THE BOILED KIDNEY...?

1-31
© King Features Syndicate, Inc., 1968. World rights reserved.

WATCH IT! SARGE HASN'T OKAYED THESE YET!
SPLOK
Mort Walker

I'M GOING DOWN FOR A BOWL OF CRUNCHIES. WOULD YOU LIKE SOME?

WELL?

I'M TRYING TO DECIDE IF THEY'RE WORTH PUTTING IN MY TEETH FOR
2/28

NO WRESTLING...
NO FOOTBALL...
NO WAR MOVIES...

HEY! WHAT'S THIS?
MORT WALKER

CLEAR THE STREET!
GO HOME, YA BUM!
ARREST HIM!
AH...A PEACE MARCH

HOW ARE THE MEATBALLS, BEETLE?

THIS ONE'S KIND OF DEAD
© King Features Syndicate, Inc., 1967. World rights reserved.
5-8
MORT WALKER

I'LL BET NOBODY IN CAMP SWAMPY CAN READ FASTER THAN PLATO
MAYBE NOBODY IN THE WHOLE WORLD

HMMM... "POWER LONGFLIGHT NUMBER TWO"
WAK
MORT WALKER

ONLY ONE DOUGH-NUT LEFT
I'LL FLIP YOU FOR IT

OKAY. I'LL TAKE HEADS
7-3
MORT WALKER

FLIP

I DON'T FEEL SO GOOD TODAY, SARGE. I TOSSED AND TURNED ALL NIGHT
OH, YEAH?! ROLL CALL IN FIVE MINUTES, BEETLE!

IT'S HARD TO LOOK SICK IN STAY-PRESSED PAJAMAS
MORT WALKER

MEN, THE CHAPLAIN IS VERY BUSY TODAY, BUT HE PROMISED TO DROP OVER AND GIVE US A COUPLE OF WORDS

BE GOOD!
Mort WALKER

WELL, THAT ABOUT WINDS UP TODAY'S MEETING ---

I TOLD YOU, BEETLE! NO CRACKS ABOUT YOUR SORE FEET BECAUSE I GOT LOST ON THE HIKE
DID I SAY ANYTHING?

DID I SAY ONE WORD?
© King Features Syndicate, Inc., 1967. World rights reserved.
MORT WALKER
11-2

MOM AND DAD THINK MY SKIRT IS TOO SHORT. DO YOU THINK IT'S TOO SHORT, KILLER?
NOO-OO-OO!

HOW ABOUT BORROWING YOUR CAR TONIGHT, FOLKS?
NOO-OO-OO!
MORT WALKER
4-12
© King Features Syndicate, Inc., 1967. World rights reserved.

IS GENERAL HALFTRACK IN?
YES. DO YOU WANT TO SEE HIM?
3-27

UH-- IS HE IN A GOOD MOOD?
WELL, YES.-
MORT WALKER

..IN A WAY
STOP THAT!
KITCHIE KITCHIE
© King Features Syndicate, Inc., 1968. World rights reserved.

HALT! WHO'S THERE?
SOPHIA LOREN
4-9

THAT'S BEETLE DOING ONE OF HIS IMPERSONATIONS. BUT IT SURE SOUNDED LIKE SOPHIA LOREN
© King Features Syndicate, Inc., 1968. World rights reserved.
MORT WALKER

TURN SIDEWAYS

SARGE'S SANDWICH HAS TO BE JUST RIGHT BEFORE HE'LL EAT IT

YEAH--BUT REARRANGING THE CARAWAY SEEDS IN HIS RYE BREAD?!
MORT WALKER
© King Features Syndicate, Inc., 1967. World rights reserved.
11-7

NEED ANY HELP, SERGEANT?
YEAH, HA! HA! HOW ARE YOU AT FIXING LOOSE TANK TREADS? (CHUCKLE)
7-12

IT'S AMAZING WHAT THEY CAN DO WITH A HAIRPIN
MORT WALKER

WHO WANTS A SODA FROM THE MACHINE?
I DO
ME TOO

LET'S SEE... ONE..TWO-- THREE--FOUR..
© King Features Syndicate, Inc., 1968. World rights reserved.

--FIVE...
MORT WALKER
4-29

I'M UP! SOMEBODY TOSS ME A BAT!
SNAP!

MORT WALKER
5-20

SEE? I TOLD YOU THERE WASN'T A BRIDGE HERE
THAT'S OKAY. WE CAN JUMP IT, BEETLE
4-1

I DON'T THINK I CAN MAKE IT, SARGE
IF YOUR FAT OLD SERGEANT CAN MAKE IT, SURELY YOU CAN!

OKAY, IF YOU PUT IT THAT WAY--
OF COURSE, I HAVEN'T TRIED IT YET--
MORT WALKER
© King Features Syndicate, Inc., 1968. World rights reserved.

GOOF-OFF!!
4-25

FINISHED?
YEAH
MORT WALKER

I DON'T TAKE THAT STUFF LYING DOWN

HE STEPPED OUT FOR A MOMENT. IF IT'S IMPORTANT I'LL GIVE HIM A MESSAGE
11-3

THE SNACK BAR JUST GOT IN TWO GALLONS OF TUTTI-FRUTTI
© King Features Syndicate, Inc., 1967. World rights reserved.
MORT WALKER

HOW ABOUT A GAME OF CHECKERS ?
HOW CAN YOU THINK ABOUT CHECKERS WHEN THE WORLD IS IN CHAOS?
3-26

YOU SHOULD AT LEAST SPEND A LITTLE TIME ON SOME OF THE GREAT PROBLEMS FACING THIS NATION AND WHAT MOVES WE SHOULD MAKE IN THE FUTURE

HOW ABOUT A GAME OF CHINESE CHECKERS?
MORT WALKER
© King Features Syndicate, Inc., 1968. World rights reserved.

I ALWAYS LOOK FORWARD TO OUR ANNUAL BIVOUAC IN THE WOODS
ME TOO. I THINK THE CHANGE IS GOOD FOR EVERYONE

MORT WALKER
10-26
© King Features Syndicate, Inc., 1967. World rights reserved.

IT'S YOUR TURN TO TRY DRILLING THE TROOPS, ZERO. DON'T BE AFRAID
OKAY--- COMP'NY, ATTEN-SHUN!
5-7

FOR-WARD.. HALT!
MORT WALKER

I FIGURE YOU CAN'T GO WRONG WITH "HALT"
© King Features Syndicate, Inc., 1968. World rights reserved.

YOU
!!GOLDBRICK!

WHY DON'T YOU SHARPEN UP, BEETLE? AREN'T YOU SICK OF HIM YELLING AT YOU?
OH, I DUNNO.. IT CLEARS UP MY DANDRUFF
© King Features Syndicate, Inc., 1967. World rights reserved.
MORT WALKER
9-18

BEETLE TOLD ME YOU WERE SICK AND I RUSHED RIGHT OVER, SARGE
THANKS, ZERO

GOLLY! IT **DOES** SOUND LIKE A WAR MOVIE!

YAWN!
4 A.M.--TIME TO WAKE BEETLE UP FOR K.P. AGAIN
I REALLY DREAD THIS! HE PUTS UP SUCH A STRUGGLE!
CQ
4-23

I HAVE TO DRAG BEETLE OUT OF BED--FIGHT WITH HIM--
TRY TO KEEP HIM QUIET--FIND HIS SOCKS FOR HIM --AND PUSH HIM TO THE MESS HALL
CQ
MORT WALKER

ZERO, TIME FOR K.P.
OKAY
© King Features Syndicate, Inc., 1968. World rights reserved.

I WONDER WHAT THOSE BIG SHOTS DO IN THEIR OFFICES ALL DAY?
HQ
4-15

I THINK I'LL CHECK UP ON THEM
MORT WALKER

?
?
© King Features Syndicate, Inc., 1968. World rights reserved.

HOLD UP, BEETLE
WHAT FOR ?

POPGUN INSPECTION
DIRTY!
8-7
MORT WALKER

SIR, THIS VISITOR SAYS THAT SOMEONE GRABBED HER DURING THE ALERT AND TRIED TO KISS HER
I'VE NEVER BEEN SO INSULTED
CAN YOU DESCRIBE HIM?
MP
4-17

I CERTAINLY CAN!
WAIT A SECOND-I THINK THE GENERAL SHOULD HEAR THIS
MORT WALKER

SIR...
© King Features Syndicate, Inc., 1968. World rights reserved.

© King Features Syndicate, Inc., 1968. World rights reserved.
COMPANY, ATTENTION!
SCRATCH
COFF

--ER-- SIMON SAYS ATTENTION ?!
YAWN
SCRATCH
3-25
MORT WALKER

DID SARGE COME BY HERE WITH THE BULLHORN ?
YES, SIR. SEVERAL TIMES
4-18

AND HERE HE COMES AGAIN

WILL GENERAL HALFTRACK HEAR FROM THE PENTAGON ?

WILL THE PENTAGON HEAR FROM GENERAL HALFTRACK ?
MORT WALKER

TUNE IN TOMORROW FOR ANOTHER EPISODE IN THIS GRIPPING DRAMA
© King Features Syndicate, Inc., 1968. World rights reserved.
2-29

I ASKED FOR A HAMBURGER AND A SHAKE, ZERO-- WHERE'S THE SHAKE?
2-10

MORT WALKER
© King Features Syndicate, Inc., 1967. World rights reserved.

I WANT FOOD!
BANG BANG
BANG
STOP IT, YOU BIG BABY!

THAT'S WHAT BABIES DO, YOU KNOW! THEY SIT IN THEIR HIGH-CHAIRS AND BANG ON THE TRAY!
DOES IT WORK?

WELL- I GUESS IT DOES
THAT'S WHAT I THOUGHT!
BRING ON THE CHOW.!!
BANG BANG
BANG
MORT WALKER
3-22
© King Features Syndicate, Inc., 1968. World rights reserved.

THE SENTRIES HAVE BEEN GETTING TOO LAX LATELY
I TOLD THEM TO CHALLENGE ME AND SOUND LIKE THEY MEANT IT!
SGT. OF
3-21

© King Features Syndicate, Inc., 1968. World rights reserved.
F GUA
I'LL PLAY YOU A PING-PONG MATCH FOR 25¢ ...OR ARE YOU CHICKEN?!
MORT WALKER

CAN I HAVE A BITE OF YOUR CANDY BAR ?
OKAY, BUT JUST ONE
3-18

I CAN'T SEEM TO GET AT IT. LET ME HOLD IT
NOPE. I'M HOLDING ON TO IT!

© King Features Syndicate, Inc., 1968. World rights reserved.
MORT WALKER

YOU OFFICERS ARE ALL OVERWEIGHT! YOU SHOULD ALL REDUCE!
LOOK AT ME! MY WAISTLINE HASN'T CHANGED IN 25 YEARS! I CAN STILL WEAR ALL MY WORLD WAR II STUFF -- SAME PANTS -- SAME BELT --
3-13

SAME RANK..
MORT WALKER
© King Features Syndicate, Inc., 1968. World rights reserved.

The affair at the EM Club was a huge success until General Halftrack's long-winded, corny speech broke up what had been a pleasant evening.

HOW DARE THEY SAY SUCH THINGS ABOUT ME IN PRINT!
3-5

WHO DO THEY THINK I AM... THE PRESIDENT?
MORT WALKER
US

THAT'S FUNNY— I THOUGHT I JUST SAW BEETLE OUTSIDE PLAYING FOOTBALL
WELL, YOU KNOW **BEETLE...**

WHEN HE FADES BACK TO PASS HE REALLY **FADES**
Z
MORT WALKER
1-30

HOW COME I CAN NEVER TELL THE DIFFERENCE BETWEEN YOUR VEGETABLE SOUP AND YOUR BEEF SOUP?

THERE REALLY ISN'T MUCH DIFFERENCE
© King Features Syndicate, Inc., 1968. World rights reserved.
MORT WALKER

IT BECOMES BEEF SOUP IF HE GETS HIS THUMB IN IT
3-6

THE GENERAL IS INSPECTING TODAY AND **EVERYONE** WILL WEAR TIES
NUTS
6-11

DIDN'T YOU BRING YOUR TIE?
I DON'T EVEN **OWN** A TIE
MORT WALKER

IT'S A LONG HIKE DOWN TO HEADQUARTERS. CAN I TAKE THE JEEP?
THAT DEPENDS ON HOW WELL YOU FIXED THE BRAKES
11-27
© King Features Syndicate, Inc., 1967. World rights reserved.

MORT WALKER

DURN BURN THAT GOOF-OFF!! CAN'T FOLLOW THROUGH ON THE SIMPLEST JOB!!
WHAT DID YOU ASK HIM TO DO?
7-8
© King Features Syndicate, Inc., 1965. World rights reserved.

MAYBE YOU EXPECT TOO MUCH OF HIM
MORT WALKER

YOU LOST YOUR MAP, SIR ?
YES. I'LL HAVE TO DO THE BEST I CAN WITH SGT. SNORKEL'S MAP
6-5

"A" COMPANY WILL RECONNOITER THE AREA COVERED BY THE BANANA BLOB, THEN MOVE ALONG THE JELLY SMEAR AND ATTACK THE COFFEE RING...
MORT WALKER
© King Features Syndicate, Inc., 1968. World rights reserved.

IT'S NO USE KIDDING MYSELF - SARGE IS THE BOSS AROUND HERE
I'M THE LIEUTENANT AND HE'S ONLY SERGEANT, BUT HE'S THE BOSS
5-28

BUT, BY GOLLY, SOME DAY THINGS WILL BE DIFFERENT! SOME DAY I'LL BE A GENERAL
BAM
MORT WALKER

IT'S NO USE KIDDING MYSELF...
© King Features Syndicate, Inc., 1968. World rights reserved.

8-3
I'M BUSHED! LET ME KNOW HOW IT TURNS OUT, ZERO

© King Features Syndicate, Inc., 1965. World rights reserved.

DURING THE TRIAL, MRS. FOSTER GETS A MYSTERIOUS MESSAGE AND DISAPPEARS. MEANWHILE, IN HIS UNDERGROUND LAB---

I'M GOING OVER TO THE TRACK MEET AND SPUR BEETLE ALONG IN THE HIGH JUMP
6-6

WHEN HIS MEN ARE COMPETING, SARGE IS ALWAYS THERE TO GIVE THEM A BOOST
MORT WALKER
© King Features Syndicate, Inc., 1968. World rights reserved.

I WONDER WHY COOKIE GOES UP ON THE ROOF TO SULK WHEN WE GRIPE ABOUT HIS FOOD?
I GUESS IT SUBCONSCIOUSLY MAKES HIM FEEL ALOOF
5-17

AND THE HEIGHT COULD BE SYMBOLIC OF THE SUPERIORITY HE WANTS TO ATTAIN
MORT WALKER

ALSO HE CAN SPIT ON US

HERE, BEETLE, TAKE THESE MEATBALLS RIGHT OVER TO SARGE
OOPS!
© King Features Syndicate, Inc., 1968. World rights reserved.

DARN! THEY FELL RIGHT IN THE MUD
I HOPE YOU CAN FIND THEM OR HE'LL BE MAD
MORT WALKER
6-10

THE MAN SAID FIRST A YELLOW PILL, THEN A BLUE PILL AND TOMORROW-- PRESTO!
THAT'S RIDICULOUS
5-21

GO AHEAD, LAUGH-- BUT IN THE MORNING YOU'LL SEE **HAIR**

OR WAS IT THE BLUE PILL, **THEN** THE YELLOW PILL?...
MORT WALKER
© King Features Syndicate, Inc., 1968. World rights reserved.

NICE-LOOKING REPORT LT. FUZZ SENT IN
YEAH
6-7

ALL OFFICIAL-- NICE COVER...NEATLY TYPED...
YEAH..

--ON THE SUBJECT OF WHO SHOULD GET TO CONTROL THE AIR-CONDITIONER SETTING IN THE "A" COMPANY ORDERLY ROOM.
MORT WALKER

NO, NO, ZERO! I TOLD YOU TO SCOUT IN **THIS** DIRECTION!
CAN'T YOU GET ANYTHING STRAIGHT FOR **ONCE?**
5-15

MORT WALKER
© King Features Syndicate, Inc., 1968. World rights reserved.

5-13

MORT WALKER

CAUTION:
FALLING
ROCK

BEETLE, ARE YOU SURE YOU GOT MY MOTOR TUNED ?
SURE! DID YOU EXPECT IT TO PLAY "THE CAISSONS GO ROLLING ALONG?"
6-19

YOU HADDA OPEN YOUR BIG MOUTH, DIDN'T YOU?
MORT WALKER
© King Features Syndicate, Inc., 1968. World rights reserved.

WHAT KIND OF A BLIND DATE DID YOU FIND FOR MY ROOM-MATE?
WELL, DOES SHE LIKE TALL HANDSOME GUYS WITH A LOT OF MONEY WHO ARE GOOD DANCERS ?
6-18

YES!
AND DOES SHE HAVE A SENSE OF HUMOR ?
MORT WALKER
© King Features Syndicate, Inc., 1962. World rights reserved.

TRY THOSE GLASSES, COOKIE, AND SEE IF THINGS LOOK ANY DIFFERENT TO YOU
OKAY, DOC
A
CLFN

HMMM--- I THINK I **CAN** SEE A **LITTLE** BETTER...
MESS HALL
MORT WALKER
5-14

AAGGGH!

HOME SWEET HOME
THE PICTURES IN THESE MAGAZINES ALMOST DRIVE ME INSANE
5-30

AT TIMES LIKE THIS THE CHAPLAIN ALWAYS HAS SOME ADVICE
© King Features Syndicate, Inc., 1968. World rights reserved.
MORT WALKER

RUN AROUND THE BLOCK, TAKE A COLD SHOWER, AND TRY TO FORGET ABOUT APPLE PIE

THAT
LT. FUZZ
IS...
SHHH, SIR.
HE'S STANDING
RIGHT OVER
THERE
6-20

HE
CAN'T
HEAR
US
YES
HE
CAN,
SIR

I CAN TELL
BY HIS
EXPRESSION
MORT
WALKER

GLORIA, PLATO IS HERE, AND HE GOT YOU A BLIND DATE
GOOD. WHO DID HE GET?
6-27

HIS NAME IS KILLER. HAVE YOU EVER HEARD OF HIM ?

YES!
© King Features Syndicate, Inc., 1968. World rights reserved.
MORT WALKER

DID I DO THAT? GOOD GRAVY! I DESERVE ANY-THING YOU DISH OUT, SARGE!

I'M A COOKED GOOSE-YOU'LL MAKE MINCEMEAT OUT OF ME--- YOU'LL SMASH ME UP LIKE HAMBURGER
7-25

FLATTER THAN A PANCAKE

YOU'VE JUST SEEN A MASTER AT WORK
MESS HALL
MORT WALKER

GENERAL! YOU SHOULDN'T BE SHARPENING YOUR OWN PENCIL!
TUT-TUT! JUST BECAUSE I'M A GENERAL DOESN'T MEAN I'M HELPLESS!
5-16

MAYBE HE HAS A POINT, THOUGH
MORT WALKER

I'LL PROBABLY FEEL THAT IN THE MORNING

DO YOU SEE THE LIFEGUARD AROUND ANYWHERE, MISS?
NO
7-18

GOOD!
MORT WALKER

ALL RIGHT, ZERO. WHAT IS IT THIS TIME?
7-17

WHY IS IT WE SCRUB **DOWN** BUT WE CLEAN **UP?**

I DON'T EVEN KNOW HOW TO LOOK THAT UP

WE'VE BEEN OUT OF THE OFFICE FOUR SECONDS AND I BET BEETLE'S ASLEEP ALREADY
OH, C'MON! **NOBODY** FALLS ASLEEP **THAT** FAST!
BESIDES, LOOK WHERE HE WAS

BET YOU A QUARTER
OKAY

Z
MORT WALKER
12-7

I TOLD YOU TO GO TO WAREHOUSE NUMBER THREE, BEETLE!!
7-24

DO YOU HAVE TO YELL INTO THE PHONE LIKE THAT, SARGE?
I GUESS I DO THAT WHEN I'M TALKING TO DUMBHEADS WHO DON'T GET THINGS STRAIGHT, SIR
MORT WALKER

I'M READY FOR THAT CALL TO SGT. SNORKEL NOW, MISS BLIPS
COTTON
© King Features Syndicate, Inc., 1968. World rights reserved.

WOW! THE WAY THOSE SKIRTS ARE GOING THEY'LL BE **GONE** BY THE END OF THE YEAR!

65...66...67... 68...
MORT WALKER
© King Features Syndicate, Inc., 1968. World rights reserved.

HEY! WHERE Y'GOING, LT. FUZZ ?
RUNNING A MILE EVERY MORNING.. IMPRESS THE GENERAL
7-23

THUNK

A TWO-MINUTE MILE! NOW **I'M** IMPRESSED!
MORT WALKER

5-24

SGT. SNORKEL'S
CHOW SURVEY

IT'S HIS
BIRTHDAY
EL'S
EY
MORT
WALKER
© King Features Syndicate, Inc., 1962, World rights reserved.

LET'S GO WATCH THE BALL GAME ON TV, SARGE
WHY? WILL JOE DIMAGGIO BE PLAYING? WILL BOBO NEWSOME BE PITCHING?

WILL THEY HAVE HANK GREENBERG OR LUKE APPLING OR STAN MUSIAL OR TED WILLIAMS OR BOBBY DOERR OR SPUD CHANDLER OR MEL OTT?
8-6

WHAT'S MORE, HE WON'T LISTEN TO ANY RECORDS BUT GLENN MILLER AND MARIO LANZA
MORT WALKER

BEETLE, I WANT THOSE WINDOWS SO CLEAN I WON'T EVEN KNOW A WINDOW'S **THERE!**
ALL RIGHT! ALL RIGHT!

HEY! ARE YOU GUYS THROUGH ALREA—
CRACK
MORT WALKER
© King Features Syndicate, Inc., 1968. World rights reserved.
9-2

TAKE A CARD, BEETLE. ANY CARD

DON'T LET ME SEE IT -- NOW PUT IT BACK
© King Features Syndicate, Inc., 1967. World rights reserved.

IT'S DITCH-DIGGING, RIGHT?
IT'S ALSO A DIRTY TRICK!
DITCH DIGGING
MORT WALKER
2-20

NOW, WHERE'S MY WALLET? I CAN'T GO TO THE MOVIES WITHOUT MY WALLET
DIDN'T YOU HIDE IT INSIDE YOUR PILLOW CASE?

OH, YEAH, THAT'S RIGHT

I THOUGHT BEETLE WAS GOING TO THE MOVIES
HE TOUCHED HIS PILLOW
Z
MORT WALKER

I TOLD SARGE' TO HAVE THIS OFFICE CLEANED UP

BEETLE! COME IN HERE!
6-17
© King Features Syndicate, Inc., 1963. World rights reserved.

IF I WANT ANYTHING DONE AROUND HERE I GOTTA DO IT **MYSELF**
MORT WALKER

JUST BECAUSE NO ONE RAVED ABOUT DINNER, HE'S SULKING AGAIN
SENSITIVE PEOPLE NEED ENCOURAGEMENT

COME ON DOWN, COOKIE! YOUR DINNER TONIGHT WAS A MASTER-PIECE! YOU'RE ONE OF THE GREAT ALL-TIME ARMY COOKS! WE ALL LOVE YOU!

KISS ME
MORT WALKER

THE GENERAL IS RIGHT. A MILE RUN IN THE MORNING GETS YOU STARTED FOR YOUR DAY'S WORK.

MORT WALKER

MISS BLIPS, CANCEL ALL MY APPOINTMENTS FOR TODAY
© King Features Syndicate, Inc., 1968. World rights reserved.

HEY! SOMEONE IS PROWLING AROUND THE MESS TENT!
CAREFUL! IT MAY BE AN OFFICER
10-2

© King Features Syndicate, Inc., 1962. World rights reserved.
DON'T SHOOT! I'LL LEAVE!

WELL, WAS IT AN OFFICER ?
HE DIDN'T SAY
MORT WALKER

6-28
YOU CAN'T CRITICIZE **MY** PIE AND GET AWAY WITH IT!

OH, NO?!

BY GOLLY, HE WAS RIGHT! IT **DOES** NEED MORE SUGAR
© King Features Syndicate, Inc., 1968. World rights reserved.
MORT WALKER

SOME SCOUTS! WE'RE SURROUNDED!
DIDN'T YOU SEE ANYTHING?!
6-29

WELL, WE SAW A FEW SPECIMENS OF RIALTO FUNGI, A CRESCENT MONARCH, SOME MUMFROID PERCANTILLOS, A HORNED LAZARUS...
YEAH!
MORT WALKER

I THINK I'VE MADE MYSELF VERY CLEAR. ARE THERE ANY QUESTIONS ?

WHAT THE GENERAL MEANT WAS--
12-8
MORT WALKER

ZERO, I TOLD YOU TO STAY OUT OF TROUBLE!
I KNOW. SO I JUST SAT HERE AND WAITED

BUT YOU **HAD** TO TRY TWIDDLING YOUR FINGERS, DIDN'T YOU?
MORT WALKER

COME WITH US TO THE DANCE, SARGE
WE'LL FIND YOU A PRETTY GIRL
I'M NOT GONNA SHAVE, SHOWER AND GET DRESSED UP FOR ANY GIRL
9-18

HOW WAS THE DANCE? I THOUGHT I'D JOIN YOU GUYS FOR A HAMBURGER
MORT WALKER
© King Features Syndicate, Inc., 1968. World rights reserved.

"What is the difference between an elephant and an orange?"
"I don't know."
"I'll never send you to the store for a dozen oranges!"
JOKES + RIDDL

ZERO, WHAT IS THE DIFFERENCE BETWEEN AN ELEPHANT AND AN ORANGE?
AN ELEPHANT IS BIGGER! RIGHT?
3-20
MORT WALKER

THEY'RE DIFFERENT COLORS! RIGHT?

(c) King Features Syndicate, Inc., 1963. World rights reserved.
ONE IS AN ANIMAL! RIGHT?

I'VE NOTICED A LOT OF SWEARING AMONG THE MEN, AND I WANT IT STOPPED!
9-19

I HOPE THAT ALL YOU OFFICERS WILL SPEAK TO YOUR TROOPS ABOUT THIS
MORT WALKER

AND SEE IF YOU CAN DO IT WITHOUT SWEARING

BOY! THOSE NEW JETS ARE FAST!
WHOOSH
ALL YOU HEAR IS A WHOOSH AND THEY'RE GONE
10-14

YOU GOTTA LOOK UP FAST OR YOU'LL MISS THEM
WHOOSH
MORT WALKER

WHOOSH

PLEASE, SARGE? PLEASE?! I'VE GOTTA HAVE A PASS TO TOWN!!
LOOK, BEETLE, I'VE TOLD YOU "NO" ABOUT FIVE HUNDRED TIMES
9-9

BUT YOU ONLY HEARD HALF MY REASONS-- NOW, ANOTHER REASON IS --
ALL RIGHT, HERE! GOLLY, I'VE NEVER SEEN SUCH PERSISTENCE!

© King Features Syndicate, Inc., 1968. World rights reserved.
CAN I HAVE TWO ?
MORT WALKER

CLICK

I'LL TAKE THREE 8X 10'S
MORT WALKER

GROWL
10-10

COOKIE!

© King Features Syndicate, Inc., 1968. World rights reserved.

THANK YOU
MORT WALKER
CHOCO DROPS

GOT THOSE CANS HOSED OUT, BEETLE?
YEAH. WHAT'LL I DO NEXT?
3-6

LOOK AROUND. THERE'S ALWAYS **SOMETHING** AROUND A MESS HALL THAT NEEDS CLEANING!
© King Features Syndicate, Inc., 1967. World rights reserved.

MORT WALKER

IT WAS HARD GETTING AWAY FROM SARGE
I THINK HE'D REALLY LIKE TO COME FOR DINNER SOMETIME
WELL, MAYBE WE'LL INVITE HIM SOMETIME

WHEN?
MORT WALKER
8-28
© King Features Syndicate, Inc., 1968. World rights reserved.

DID YOU SCRUB OUT ALL THOSE GARBAGE CANS REAL GOOD, BEETLE?
YEAH... CAN I GO NOW, COOKIE?
11-4

WE'LL SEE
MORT WALKER

HEY, SARGE, THOSE TWO KIDS WHO HANG AROUND THE FENCE JUST CLIMBED IN
DURN BURN 'EM!
8-15

THEY STARTED RUNNING AROUND THE OBSTACLE COURSE
DURN BURN EM!!
© King Features Syndicate, Inc., 1968. World rights reserved.

THEY BEAT OUR BEST TIME
DURN BURN 'EM!!!
MORT WALKER

OKAY, LET'S GET THIS PLACE CLEANED UP!
WHY?
2-6

ONE MORE WORD, BEETLE, AND I'LL CLEAN UP THIS BARRACKS WITH **YOU!**
DON'T MAKE ME LAUGH!

© King Features Syndicate, Inc., 1967. World rights reserved.
MORT WALKER

I DIDN'T THINK THE ARMY WOULD ALLOW PUNISHMENT LIKE THIS IN THIS DAY AND AGE!
NEITHER DID I
8-20

FRANKLY, I THINK HE'S BLUFFING
MORT WALKER

HEY, PLATO! DID YOU SEE THE CHORUS GIRLS FOR THE SHOW TONIGHT GO BY?!
YEAHHH

THERE'S KILLER! I WONDER IF HE SAW THEM!
HEY, KILLER!

HE SAW THEM
MORT WALKER
4-4
© King Features Syndicate, Inc., 1967. World rights reserved.

CAUTION
WATCH YOUR SPEED

MORT WALKER
8-7

WELL, I CAN'T DO **EVERYTHING!**

THERE! SEE THOSE RED SPOTS, DOCTOR?
YES. HMMM
4-7

STRANGE. NOW THEY'RE GONE!
© 1961, King Features Syndicate, Inc., World rights reserved.

NOW THEY'RE BACK AGAIN!! YOU MUST BE VERY ALLERGIC TO SOMETHING!
MORT WALKER

HOW DO YOU LIKE MY NEW SUIT, KILLER?
HMMM.. STAND UP
5-18

UH-HUH.. NOW TURN AROUND

SNEEZE
MORT WALKER

THIS IS A LOUSY CAMPSITE YOU FOUND, SARGE
WELL, IF ANY OF YOU THINK YOU CAN FIND A BETTER ONE, HOP IN!

MORT WALKER
© King Features Syndicate, Inc., 1968, World rights reserved.
8-27

AS IF WE WEREN'T HAVING ENOUGH TROUBLE! NOW **HE** SHOWS UP!
WELL, THAT'S A GENERAL'S FUNCTION
WHAT'S A GENERAL'S FUNCTION ?
9-12

TO GET THINGS ALL FOULED UP AND THEN RUSH IN TO STRAIGHTEN THINGS OUT
CAN'T FOLLOW SIMPLE ORDERS!
HMPH!
HERE, I'LL TAKE OVER!
MORT WALKER

SEE IF YOU CAN KILL THAT FLY.
BUT DON'T MAKE ANY LOUD NOISES... THE CAPTAIN'S TAKING A NAP

HERE HE IS, SARGE-- HE'S STILL ALIVE
WHAT DO YOU WANT **ME** TO DO WITH HIM?
1-14

BREATHE ON HIM
MORT WALKER
© King Features Syndicate, Inc., 1967. World rights reserved.

WOW! 48... 49... 50!
WHOSE BIRTHDAY?!
MORT WALKER

IT'S MY MATTRESS'S
7-11
© King Features Syndicate, Inc., 1967. World rights reserved.

BOY! I'LL NEVER FORGET THAT SWINGING BEACH PARTY WE HAD LAST WEEK
YEAH!
MORT WALKER

NEITHER WILL THE GENERAL
OFF LIMITS!
© King Features Syndicate, Inc., 1968. World rights reserved.
8-29